To:

From:

My favorite recipes are:

INDEX

Desserts
Baked Apples..6
Baked Bananas...9
Fresh Peach Pie...3
Frosted Watermelon Delight...................................10
Healthy Champagne Delight.....................................8
Lemon Ice Cream Dessert.......................................7
Melon Delight...1
Peanut Butter Honey Delites...................................2
Spicy Pears..11
Whipped Honey Lemon Yogurt....................................4
Yogurt-Sauced Peaches...5

Poultry
American Turkey Pie..44
Chickenburgers American Style................................23
Chicken Casserole..31

Chicken Continental 38
Chicken Curry 28
Chicken in Beer 19
Chicken in Buttermilk 20
Chicken in Lemon 21
Chicken in Orange Juice 40
Chicken Livers in Yogurt 18
Chicken Loaf Ensemble 27
Chicken Marrakesh 15
Chicken Oregano 16
Chicken Paprika 32
Chicken Pineapple 34
Chicken Supreme 37
Chicken Teriyaki 36
Chicken with Mushroom Gravy 25
Cooking Chicken as Easy as Apple Pie 39
Golden Apricot Chicken Breasts 41
Island Chicken Haven 26

Italian Chicken	29
Marinated Broiled Chicken	24
Mexican Oven-Fried Chicken	33
Mozzarella Chicken	42
Shanghai Duck	12
Souper Turkey Burgers	43
Southwest Turkey Chili	30
Speedy Chicken	22
Spiced Oven-Fried Chicken	17
Turkey Broccoli Pilaf	35
Turkey Burgers Deluxe	13
Turkey Loaf Delite	14

Vegetables

Baked Corn	55
Baked Eggplant	45
Baked Green Peppers	60
Baked Rice	53
Broccoli Casserole	52

Brussels Sprouts & Mushrooms	61
Cabbage Salad	66
Copper Pennies	54
Creole Celery Delight	57
Easy Green Pea Casserole	50
Fried Okra	51
Green Bean Casserole	49
Green Beans in Mustard Sauce	64
Low Cal Green Beans	59
Peas & Celery	58
Pineapple Carrots	63
Quick Asparagus Casserole	56
Quick Broiled Zucchini with Cheese	65
Sauteed Zucchini Strips	62
Spinach	67
Stewed Tomatoes	68
Stir-Fried Cabbage	46
Stuffed Peppers	48

Vegetable Casserole 47
Salads
Asparagus-Yogurt Salad 86
Carrot-Raisin Salad 81
Cauliflower Salad 70
Chinese Salad 77
Cold Broccoli Salad 74
Corn Salad 91
Cranberry Salad 89
Cucumber Salad 73
5 Cup Salad 75
Green Salad 71
Light Fruit Salad 78
Marinated Fruit Salad 79
Pea Salad 76
Quick Potato Salad 87
Red Cabbage-Apple Slaw 84
Refreshing Yogurt Coleslaw 72

Rice Salad	82
Seven Layer Salad	80
Spinach Salad	85
Stuffed Tomato Salad	88
Summer Salad	90
Yogurt & Fruit Salad	69
Zucchini-Mushroom Salad	83

Fish/Seafood

Asparagus Filet of Sole	93
Baked Carp	100
Baked Halibut	101
Baked Mozzarella Bass	98
Baked Sole with Mushrooms	103
Baked Tuna Fish Cakes	118
Barbecued Herbed Fish	122
California Scallops	115
Crab Bisque	116
Crab "Stuffed" Flounder	120

Easy Camper Fish Dinner	92
Fillet of Sole	109
Fish Creole	127
Holly Mackerel with Yogurt & Chives	113
Italian Fish Steaks	121
Light Tuna Chef Salad	95
Low Cal Tuna Salad	111
Marinade Grilled Swordfish	104
Mozzarella Fish Delite	94
Mushroom Baked Sole	119
Orange Ruffie Fish Fillets with Pineapple	106
Oven Poached Haddock	105
Quick Broiled Fish	108
Red Snapper Filet	110
Baked Salmon Steaks	112
Tangy Fish	117
Tomato Baked Shrimp	99
Tuna Chopstick Delite	107

Tuna Tacos 96
Turbot Italiano 114
Wino Trout 102
Wisconsin Lake Trout Au Gratin 97

Soups
Appetizer Soup 123
Asparagus-Crab Soup 132
Bouillabaise Soup 125
Broccoli Soup 130
Cabbage Soup 133
Carrot Soup 134
Cucumber Soup 131
Delightful Turkey Soup 139
Farmers Stew 126
Fish Chowder 132
French Onion Soup 137
Fresh Tomato Soup 136
Homemade Chicken Stock 128

Mixed Vegetable Soup 138
Mushroom Soup 129
Potato & Leek Soup 135
Zucchini Soup 124

DESSERTS

MELON DELITE

Serves 4

Cantaloupe
1 C. pineapple juice
Watermelon
Honeydew

From each chilled melon make 1 cup melon balls. In 4 parfait glasses, alternate layers of 3 melon types. Pour pineapple juice over melon. Serve chilled.

PEANUT BUTTER HONEY DELITES

Makes 48 pieces

1 C. smooth peanut butter
1½ C. nonfat dry milk
Additional peanuts, optional for topping garnish

1 C. honey
1 C. no salt dry roasted peanuts, finely chopped

Mix smooth peanut butter, honey and dry milk until mixture is smooth. Stir in peanuts. Spread in 8" square pan. Refrigerate until firm. Cut into 48 squares and place a peanut half on each if desired. Remember each piece is 60 calories!

FRESH PEACH PIE

Serves 8

1/8 C. sugar substitute
½ C. unsweetened white grape juice
1½ C. mashed fresh peaches
Crunchy whole wheat pastry shell
3 T. cornstarch
3 C. sliced fresh peaches

Combine sugar substitute and cornstarch in medium-size pan; stir in grape juice and mashed peaches. Bring to a boil; reduce heat and simmer about 5 minutes or until mixture thickens, stirring constantly. Remove from heat and cool. Place sliced peaches in crunchy whole wheat pastry shell. Spoon cooled peach mixture over sliced peaches. Chill overnight. Cut into 8 pieces. Watch out, each piece is 185 calories.

WHIPPED HONEY LEMON YOGURT

Serves 4

1 C. plain lowfat yogurt
Grated rind and juice
of ½ lemon
Lemon rind for top

2 T. honey, warmed
1 egg white, beaten

Mix together the yogurt, honey, lemon rind and juice. Beat the egg white until stiff and fold into yogurt mixture. Spoon into 4 glasses and top each with thin curls of lemon rind. Serve chilled. Only 60 calories per serving.

YOGURT-SAUCED PEACHES   Serves 8

¼ C. lowfat cottage cheese
1 T. sugar substitute
1/8 tsp. ground cardamon
8 fresh peaches or 2-16 oz. cans lite sliced peaches

½ C. skim milk
1 tsp. lemon juice
¾ C. plain lowfat yogurt

In blender combine cottage cheese, skim milk, sugar, lemon juice and cardamon. Cover; process till smooth; fold in yogurt. Chill. At serving time, using paring knife, peel, pit and slice peaches. If you are using canned peaches; drain. Divide peaches among 8 sherbet dishes. Spoon sauce over peaches.
NOTE: You can substitute your favorite fruit for the peaches. Only 90 calories per serving.

BAKED APPLES

Serves 4

4 baking apples, cored	4 T. clear honey
4 T. raisins	Cinnamon to taste

With a paring knife, core apples and stand them bottom down in a baking dish. Spread a thin layer of honey inside and on top of the apple. Sprinkle cinnamon to taste, making sure some gets inside the apple. Stuff raisins into the center of the apple. Bake uncovered for 20 to 30 minutes or until apple skin starts to split.

LEMON ICE CREAM DESSERT Serves 6

3 T. margarine, melted
1/8 tsp. low sodium salt
¼ C. sugar substitute
2 tsp. grated lemon rind

1 T. flour
3½ C. skim milk
½ C. lemon juice

Melt margarine in pan. Blend in flour and salt. Add half the skim milk, stirring steadily to the boiling point. Mix in sugar, then cook on low heat 5 to 10 minutes. Remove from heat and stir in remaining milk. Turn into a refrigerator tray and freeze until sides set. Turn into a bowl, add the lemon juice and rind; beat until frothy. Return to the tray and freeze until set. Only 120 calories per serving.
NOTE: When enjoying this, think you are eating your favorite ice cream without all of that fat!

HEALTHY CHAMPAGNE DELIGHT

Serves 4

8 oz. pink champagne
2 tsp. lemon juice

4 C. your favorite fresh fruit; good ones include: strawberries, peaches, blueberries
½ T. sugar substitute

Combine pieces of fruit in a bowl and sprinkle with lemon juice to prevent darkening. Sparsely sprinkle the sugar over the fruit and stir. Chill. When ready to serve divide fruit in 4 sherbet glasses. Pour chilled pink champagne over fruit. Don't go back for seconds as each serving is 210 calories!
NOTE: If you want fewer calories try using diet strawberry soda or lemon-lime soda instead of champagne; only 60 calories with diet pop per serving.

BAKED BANANAS

Serves 4

4 medium bananas
4 T. honey
4 T. lemon juice

With a knife, cut bananas lengthwise into halves. Place in ungreased baking dish. Mix lemon juice and honey separately and brush on bananas. Bake at 350° uncovered until bananas are golden, 10 to 15 minutes. 90 calories per serving.

FROSTED WATERMELON DELIGHT

Serves 8

½ watermelon
1 pt. raspberry sherbet
1 pt. fresh raspberries, washed

With serving spoon scoop meat from watermelon half in spoonfuls, reserving shell. With a paring knife remove surface seeds from watermelon with tip of knife. Return watermelon to shell, with rounded side up. Chill overnight. To serve, next day top watermelon with spoonfuls of lowfat raspberry sherbet; scatter raspberries over sherbet. Only 90 calories per serving.

SPICY PEARS

Serves 4

4 ripe pears, peeled, halved
  and cored
¼ tsp. cinnamon

2 C. cranberry juice
¼ tsp. ground cloves
Optional: ½ tsp. orange
  and lemon rind

Combine all the ingredients in a saucepan. Bring to boil; reduce heat. Cover pan and simmer pears about 20 minutes or until they are tender. Serve pears warm or chilled.

POULTRY

SHANGHAI DUCK

Serves 6

8 scallions, cut into 2" lengths
2 slices ginger root, size of half dollar
1 C. dark soy sauce, low sodium
1 C. water
2 star anise (16 sections)
1 duck (4 to 5 lbs.)
1 C. light soy sauce, low sodium
¼ C. sugar (or substitute)

Place the scallions, star anise and ginger root in a large pot or pan. Place the duck, breast side up. In separate bowl mix remaining ingredients and pour over the duck. Cover and bring to a boil. Simmer on low heat for 2 to 2½ hours or until tender; turn every hour. Cut in small pieces and serve hot.

TURKEY BURGERS DELUXE

Serves 4

1 lb. ground turkey
2 T. unsalted margarine, melted
¼ tsp. garlic powder
½ C. fine chopped white onion
1 T. lemon juice
1/8 tsp. basil leaves

Mix all ingredients thoroughly. Place into 4 patties. Set oven at broil or 550°. Cook patties 3" from heat for 3 to 4 minutes on each side for rare; 6 to 7 minutes for medium.

TURKEY LOAF DELITE

Serves 6

1 lb. ground turkey
¼ C. wheat germ
½ C. thinly sliced celery
¼ tsp. ground pepper
2 egg whites
½ C. unprocessed bran
1 clove garlic, minced
¾ C. water
2 C. chopped white onion
1 tsp. dry mustard

Heat oven to 350°. In non-stick pan or spray with vegetable spray loaf pan (9x5x3") or similar size) mix into bowl; add water and allow to stand until softened. Mix in remaining ingredients. Place in loaf pan and bake 45 minutes or until golden brown.

CHICKEN MARRAKESH

Serves 6

6 boned and skinned chicken breasts
2 tsp. pepper
1 clove garlic, minced
2/3 C. lemon juice
1/2 tsp. low sodium salt
2 T. thyme

Place chicken in a bowl. Mix together lemon juice, garlic, thyme, low sodium salt, pepper and pour over chicken. Marinate chicken in refrigerator for 4 to 6 hours. Remove chicken from marinade and place in shallow baking dish. Bake at 350° for 40 to 50 minutes or until tender.

CHICKEN OREGANO

Serves 4

4-6 oz. boneless, skinned chicken breasts
2 T. lemon juice
½ C. unsalted margarine, melted
1½ tsp. oregano
½ tsp. pepper

Broil or bake at 550°. Mix margarine, lemon juice, oregano and pepper. Lightly brush chicken with about 3 tablespoons of margarine mixture. Cook 20 to 25 minutes or until brown. Turn; brush remaining margarine mixture and cook 20 to 25 minutes or until tender.

SPICED OVEN-FRIED CHICKEN

Serves 4 to 6

3 lb. fryer, cut up
¼ tsp. garlic powder
2 tsp. curry powder
¼ C. skim milk
¼ tsp. paprika
2 T. minced white onion
½ tsp. dry mustard
¼ tsp. low sodium salt
1 C. dry whole wheat bread crumbs

Heat oven to 375°. Mix all ingredients except chicken and milk. Dip chicken pieces in milk, then coat with crumb mixture. Place chicken in non-stick pan or spray pan with vegetable oil. Oven bake for 60 to 70 minutes or until tender and juicy.

CHICKEN LIVERS IN YOGURT

Serves 4

1½ lbs. chicken livers	1 C. clear canned, less salt, chicken broth
½ C. chopped mushrooms	½ tsp. low sodium salt
1 clove garlic, minced	¼ tsp. pepper
3 T. unsalted margarine	1 C. plain lowfat yogurt
¼ tsp. basil	

Cut livers in 2 at the natural separation. Place in non-stick skillet or spray with vegetable oil and saute 3 to 4 minutes with medium heat or until golden. Turn heat to low and mix in all remaining ingredients except yogurt. Cook, uncovered, 8 to 12 minutes; stir occasionally. Mix in yogurt and serve over rice.

CHICKEN IN BEER

Serves 4

- 4 large boneless chicken breasts, skinned removed, each cut into 3 to 4 smaller pieces
- 2 T. low-sodium mustard
- 1 T. basil
- 1½ C. fresh sliced mushrooms
- 1 clove garlic, minced
- 1 C. no salt tomato sauce (or paste)
- 1 C. light beer
- 3 T. olive oil
- 1 C. chopped white onions

In medium-size pan saute onions and garlic in olive oil. Add fresh sliced mushrooms. Saute until tender. Add light beer, tomato sauce and spices. Add chicken pieces. Cover pan and simmer on low heat for 30 to 35 minutes or until tender.

CHICKEN IN BUTTERMILK

Serves 6

4 lbs. chicken broilers, skinned removed
1½ C. chopped white onions
½ tsp. pepper
2 T. curry powder
2 T. vegetable oil
¼ tsp. low sodium salt
2 cloves garlic, minced
1 C. 1% buttermilk

Marinate chicken for 2 hours in a mixture of buttermilk, pepper, salt and garlic, turning and basting frequently. Drain chicken and reserve the marinade mixture. Heat vegetable oil in deep skillet or pan; saute the onions for 10 minutes. Mix in the curry powder; add the chicken and brown lightly. Add the marinade mixture; cover and cook on low heat 70 to 90 minutes or until tender.

CHICKEN IN LEMON

Serves 6

- 3 lbs. boneless chicken breasts, skinned
- 2 T. unsalted margarine
- 9 T. lemon juice
- ½ C. flour
- 2 T. vegetable oil
- 1 T. sugar substitute
- 1/8 C. black pepper

Mix the flour and pepper together in a bowl. Coat the chicken with the flour mixture. Heat the margarine with vegetable oil in a large frying pan. Add chicken and cook over medium heat until golden brown on both sides. Remove chicken to a platter. Mix lemon juice and sugar into the frying pan and stir frequently over low heat for 2 to 3 minutes; pour it over the cooked chicken.

SPEEDY CHICKEN

Serves 6

2 lbs. boneless chicken breasts, skinned
4 T. unsalted margarine

Optional: 4 lemon slices and chopped parsley for garnish

Cut chicken breasts into 8 to 12 strips. In skillet over medium heat, in margarine, cook chicken strips. Brown each side; cover and cook for 10 minutes or until tender.

CHICKENBURGERS AMERICAN STYLE Serves 4

1½ C. ground, cooked chicken
1 tsp. mixed dried herbs
¾ C. white onion, chopped
1 C. lowfat (1% or less milk fat) cottage cheese, unsalted, drained

Mix together chicken and onion. Pepper to taste. Add the mixed herbs, then the cottage cheese and mix well. Shape into 4 flat patties. Grill or cook each side for 5 to 7 minutes or until heated throughout.

MARINATED BROILED CHICKEN

Serves 6

4 lbs. chicken broilers, quartered and skinned
2 tsp. powdered ginger
1/2 C. chopped white onions
1/3 C. low sodium soy sauce
2 T. vegetable oil
2 T. prepared horseradish
1 T. sugar substitute
1/3 C. dry sherry

Mix together and bring to a boil the sherry, soy sauce, sugar, onions, horseradish and ginger; cook over low heat 3 minutes. Brush the chicken with the mixture and let stand 45 to 60 minutes. Oil a broiling pan with 1 tablespoon oil. Broil 15 minutes and then turn. Brush on the remaining oil and broil 15 minutes longer or until tender and juicy; basting frequently.

CHICKEN WITH MUSHROOM GRAVY　　　　　　Serves 6

- 6 boneless chicken breasts, skinned
- 2 tsp. cornstarch
- ½ tsp. low sodium salt
- 1 C. mushroom stems and pieces, drained
- 1½ C. no salt tomato juice
- ¼ tsp. garlic powder
- ½ C. chopped white onions
- 2 T. water
- 1 tsp. basil leaves

Coat skillet with vegetable spray. Brown chicken over medium heat. Pour tomato juice over chicken. Mix in onion, salt, basil leaves and garlic powder. Cover and simmer 55 to 70 minutes or until tender. Stir in mushroom stems and pieces. Mix cornstarch and water; stir liquid in skillet. Cook, stirring constantly, until mixture thickens and boils. Boil and stir 1 minute.

ISLAND CHICKEN HAVEN

Serves 4

2 large boneless skinned chicken breasts, halved
¼ tsp. ground pepper
1 C. pineapple chunks in unsweetened pineapple juice
½ tsp. Tabasco sauce
3 T. unsalted margarine
2 medium-size green peppers, cut into thin strips
2½ T. lime juice
Cooked rice

Melt margarine in skillet. Place chicken breasts in skillet; season with pepper. Brown chicken over medium heat about 10 minutes. Turn chicken; season with pepper and brown for 10 minutes. Add green pepper and pineapple chunks (with juice) and heat to boiling. Mix lime juice and Tabasco sauce; pour on chicken. Cover and simmer over low heat for 15 minutes or until tender. Serve with rice.

CHICKEN LOAF ENSEMBLE

Serves 6 to 8

5 lbs. chicken, cut into small pieces
3 C. clear, less salt, chicken broth

4 egg whites, well beaten
1 C. celery, chopped fine
2 C. cracker crumbs, not too fine (also may use 2 C. whole wheat bread crumbs)

Mix all together; put in non-stick loaf pan or spray pan with vegetable spray. Bake for 35 to 45 minutes.

CHICKEN CURRY

Serves 6

6 boneless and skinned chicken breasts, cut into bite-size pieces
2 T. unsalted margarine
1 C. chopped white onion
2 C. tomatoes (no salt), chopped
1 clove garlic, minced
¾ C. chopped green pepper
2 T. olive oil
2 tsp. curry powder
¼ tsp. thyme

In a large skillet saute chicken in olive oil until chicken is cooked. Remove chicken to platter. Melt margarine in same skillet. Saute onion, garlic and green peppers until soft. Blend in curry powder and thyme. Add chicken and stir until well coated with sauce. Mix in tomatoes.

ITALIAN CHICKEN

Serves 8

8 boneless and skinned chicken breasts
1 C. marinara sauce or oil-free Italian sauce
1 white onion, sliced
6 T. grated Parmesan cheese

Place chicken in baking dish and cover with onion slices. Top with Italian sauce and sprinkle with Parmesan cheese. Cover; bake at 350° for 40 to 45 minutes or until tender.

SOUTHWEST TURKEY CHILI

Serves 8

2 lbs. ground turkey
2 cloves garlic, minced
2 green peppers, chopped
3 C. cooked kidney beans
2 cans no salt tomato paste
5 T. mild chili powder
4 T. diced green chili peppers
1 C. clear, less salt, chicken broth
3 cans no salt added whole tomatoes
2 T. hot chili powder
2 T. cumin
3 white onions, chopped

Brown ground turkey in a non-stick skillet or spray skillet with vegetable spray; drain off any fat. Brown onions, peppers and garlic in chicken broth. Mix together cooked beans, tomatoes, other spices and ground turkey. Don't worry about any leftovers as this chili is even better the second day.

CHICKEN CASSEROLE

Serves 4

2 large boneless, skinned chicken breasts
1-8 oz. can no salt green peas
2 chicken bouillon cubes
1-16 oz. can French-style green beans
1 lb. sliced fresh mushrooms
¼ C. low sodium soy sauce
1 C. water

Preheat oven to 350°. Arrange chicken and vegetables in pan. Dissolve bouillon in hot water and blend in soy sauce. Pour over chicken and vegetables. Let stand 5 minutes before baking. Bake for 30 to 35 minutes or until tender.

CHICKEN PAPRIKA

Serves 4

2 lbs. boneless, skinned chicken breasts
2 white onions, thinly sliced
1 T. cornstarch
1 C. no salt tomato juice
½ C. plain lowfat yogurt
4 T. unsalted margarine
1 T. paprika
1½ C. hot cooked noodles

In skillet over medium heat brown chicken in margarine about 20 minutes. Remove chicken to platter. Add onions to skillet; cook till tender. Drain. Mix tomato juice and paprika into skillet. Add chicken; cover and cook for 40 to 45 minutes. Remove chicken to platter. Skim any fat from pan juices! Stir cornstarch into yogurt. Stir ½ cup pan juices into yogurt mixture; return all to skillet. Cook on low heat till thickened. Serve chicken and sauce with noodles.

MEXICAN OVEN-FRIED CHICKEN

Serves 6

3 lbs. boneless, skinned chicken breasts
1 C. crushed cornflakes cereal
1 tsp. chili powder
¼ tsp. garlic powder
2 C. Bloody Mary mix
½ tsp. ground cumin
½ tsp. onion salt

Combine chicken and Bloody Mary mix in large pan or bowl; cover and refrigerate overnight. Mix together all remaining ingredients the next day. Drain chicken and coat in cereal mixture. In non-stick pan, or spray pan with vegetable spray, bake in 350° oven for 55 to 65 minutes or until tender.

CHICKEN PINEAPPLE

Serves 8

4 to 5 lbs. broiler fryers, quartered and skinned
½ tsp. ground ginger
1-20 oz. can sliced pineapple, packed in water
¼ C. no salt soy sauce
½ tsp. garlic powder
2 tsp. instant minced onion

Preheat oven to 375°. Drain pineapple and reserve ¼ cup pineapple juice. Mix pineapple juice, soy sauce, onion, ginger and garlic powder in roasting pan. Add chicken and bake 60 to 65 minutes or until tender. Add sliced pineapple and bake an additional 5 minutes.

TURKEY-BROCCOLI PILAF

Serves 4

- 2 C. clear, less salt, chicken broth
- ½ C. chopped onion
- 1-10 oz. pkg. frozen cut broccoli
- 2 T. slivered almonds, toasted
- 1 tsp. thyme
- ½ C. brown rice
- 1/8 tsp. pepper
- 3 C. cooked turkey, cut into strips

In a saucepan, bring the chicken broth to a boil, add the uncooked rice, onion, thyme and pepper. Reduce heat, cover and simmer 50 to 55 minutes or until rice is tender. Cook the broccoli as package directs; don't drain. Mix turkey, almonds and broccoli into cooked rice mixture. Simmer until heated through or about 10 minutes.

CHICKEN TERIYAKI

Serves 6

3 lbs. boneless, skinned chicken breasts
½ C. low sodium soy sauce
1½ C. dry white wine
½ tsp. garlic powder
½ tsp. ground ginger

Place chicken in large pan. In separate pan mix remaining ingredients; pour over chicken. Cover and refrigerate overnight. Coat pan with vegetable cooking spray. Remove chicken from marinade mixture and place in pan. Cook 15 to 20 minutes on each side; basting with any leftover marinade mixture.

CHICKEN SUPREME
Serves 8

8 boneless, skinned chicken breasts
1 can low salt cream of chicken soup
1 can water chestnuts, optional
1-12 oz. box cornflakes*
1 can low salt cream of mushroom soup
1-8 oz. lowfat plain yogurt
2 white onions, chopped

Boil chicken breasts and cut into smaller pieces. Mix soups, yogurt, onions, water chestnuts and chicken. Pour into 2-quart casserole dish. Crush cornflakes and put on top. Bake at 375° for 35 to 40 minutes.
*You may use whole wheat bread crumbs instead of cornflakes.

CHICKEN CONTINENTAL

Serves 6

- 4 lb. frying chicken, skinned and cut into pieces
- ¼ C. low salt margarine
- 1 T. chopped parsley
- 1⅓ C. water
- 1 can low salt cream of chicken soup
- 1 tsp. black pepper
- 1⅓ C. Minute rice
- ⅔ C. flour
- 1 white onion, chopped
- 1/8 tsp. thyme

Roll chicken in flour; brown in margarine. Remove chicken to platter. Stir soup, seasonings and water into drippings; cook and stir to boil. Spread Minute rice from box in 2-quart casserole dish. Pour all but ⅔ cup soup over rice; stir to moisten. Top rice with chicken and remaining soup. Bake at 375° for 35 to 40 minutes or until tender.

COOKING CHICKEN AS EASY AS APPLE PIE   Serves 4

4 boneless, skinned chicken breasts
1 C. apple cider
1½ T. cooking sherry
¾ tsp. garlic
2 large apples, cored and diced
¼ tsp. sage
1½ tsp. cinnamon

Marinate chicken in cider and sherry overnight. Remove chicken from marinade mixture and place in baking dish. Add the rest of the ingredients. Bake at 375°, uncovered, 50 to 60 minutes. Baste occasionally with juices from marinade.

CHICKEN IN ORANGE JUICE

Serves 6

6 large boneless, skinned chicken breasts
6 oz. frozen orange juice without water added
4 cloves, chopped
½ tsp. nutmeg
2 T. lemon juice
3 T. low salt margarine
2 white onions, chopped
¼ C. honey
1 tsp. ginger

Brown the chicken and onions using margarine in a large skillet. Remove from skillet and place in a baking dish without any fat. Add the rest of the ingredients and bake for 60 to 65 minutes at 375°.

GOLDEN APRICOT CHICKEN BREASTS

Serves 4

- 4 boneless, skinned chicken breasts
- 1 C. apricot preserves
- 2 tsp. dry mustard
- 4 oz. mozzarella cheese (made with part skim milk)
- 3 T. Worcestershire sauce

Using sharp knife, cut pockets in chicken breasts. Stuff cheese in pockets. Top with sauce made from apricot preserves, dry mustard and Worcestershire sauce. Bake uncovered for 60 to 65 minutes at 325°; basting as needed.

MOZZARELLA CHICKEN

Serves 6

6 boneless, skinned chicken breasts
1 can low salt cream of chicken soup
1 C. stuffing mix, crushed
6 slices lowfat mozzarella cheese
¼ C. water
1/8 C. low salt margarine

Place chicken in 9x13" pan. Top each breast with a slice of mozzarella cheese. Combine soup and water and mix well. Pour over chicken. Sprinkle stuffing mix or whole wheat crushed bread crumbs over top. Sparsely drizzle with low salt margarine. Bake 55 to 60 minutes at 375°.

SOUPER TURKEY BURGERS

Serves 4

1 lb. ground turkey
1-8 oz. can low salt vegetable
  soup
¾ C. chopped white onions
2 T. catsup
1 tsp. prepared mustard

In skillet sprayed with vegetable oil brown turkey and onions; drain any fat. Add soup, catsup, mustard and simmer about 4 minutes. Serve on whole wheat toasted buns.

AMERICAN TURKEY PIE

Serves 4

1 lb. ground turkey
1-8 oz. can tomato sauce
1 can crescent rolls
2 green peppers, chopped
2 white onions, chopped
8 oz. shredded mozzarella cheese (made with part skim milk)

Brown ground turkey; drain. Saute onions and green peppers. In bowl mix cooked turkey, onions, green peppers and tomato sauce. Unroll crescent rolls and press down in greased pie plate to form crust. Allow points of rolls to hang over sides. Add turkey mixture to dish. Sprinkle with mozzarella cheese. Fold points of rolls up over top of pie. Bake at 375° for 25 minutes.

BAKED EGGPLANT

Serves 6

- 2 eggplants
- 4 T. no salt margarine
- 2 egg whites only, well beaten
- 2 C. whole wheat bread crumbs
- 1 white onion, chopped fine
- 2 C. shredded mozzarella cheese (made with part skim milk)
- 1 tsp. sage

Cook eggplant in clear water until tender. Saute onion in no salt margarine. Dampen whole wheat bread crumbs. Drain water from eggplant and mix everything together. Put in non-stick baking dish or spray with vegetable spray and top with mozzarella cheese. Bake at 350° for 30 minutes.

STIR-FRIED CABBAGE

Serves 4

½ C. chopped white onion
1 small head cabbage or about 1 lb. shredded cabbage
1/8 tsp. dried tarragon
¼ tsp. pepper
¼ tsp. dried savory
1 T. vegetable oil

Saute onions in oil; add cabbage and stir until lightly browned. Add remaining ingredients; cover and cook until cabbage is tender, but not soggy.

VEGETABLE CASSEROLE

Serves 6

- 2 lbs. frozen mixed vegetables
- 1 can low salt cream of mushroom soup
- 1 C. whole wheat bread crumbs, optional
- 1 C. shredded mozzarella cheese (made with part skim milk)
- 2 T. no salt margarine

Cook vegetables as directed. Drain and add mushroom soup, butter and mozzarella cheese. Stir and mix well. Pour in casserole. Top with whole wheat bread crumbs if desired. Bake at 350° for 25 to 30 minutes or until it bubbles.

STUFFED PEPPERS

Serves 6

1 lb. ground turkey
1-16 oz. can tomatoes, no salt
2 cans no salt tomato sauce
1 small white onion, chopped
6 green bell peppers
Season with garlic salt and black pepper to taste
¾ C. raw rice

Mix turkey, rice, garlic salt, pepper, onion, half of tomato sauce and tomatoes. Wash and clean out peppers, drain upside down to remove any water. Stuff peppers with turkey mixture. Pour remaining tomato sauce and tomatoes. Place peppers in covered casserole. Place peppers in casserole, spooning small amount of sauce over each pepper. Bake at 350° for about 1 hour or until rice is cooked.

GREEN BEAN CASSEROLE

Serves 6

- 2 cans French-style beans (no salt added)
- 1 can low salt mushroom soup, diluted with ¾ can skim milk
- 1 can chow mein noodles
- 1 C. whole wheat bread crumbs

Put half of beans, then half of noodles and then half of soup in layers in non-stick casserole dish or spray with vegetable spray. Repeat. Bake at 400° for 30 minutes. Add bread crumbs to top of casserole before last 5 minutes of baking.

EASY GREEN PEA CASSEROLE

Serves 4

1 can no salt green peas
1 can low salt cream of mushroom soup
1 white onion, chopped

Drain peas. Mix with remaining ingredients and bake at 350° for 25 minutes.

FRIED OKRA Serves 4

8 okra Vegetable oil
1 C. corn meal Pepper to taste

Select young, tender okra about ¼" thick and 3 to 4" long. With knife, remove stems, wash and cook in boiling water until tender, about 10 to 15 minutes. Drain in colander. Season with black pepper to taste; press each okra flat and roll in meal. Fry in hot vegetable oil until brown. Drain oil and serve hot.

BROCCOLI CASSEROLE

Serves 6

2-8 oz. pkgs. frozen chopped broccoli
1 white onion, chopped
2 C. Minute rice
8 oz. shredded mozzarella cheese (made with part skim milk)
2 cans low salt cream of mushroom soup, diluted
¼ C. no salt margarine

Cook broccoli as directed on package. Saute onion in no salt margarine or vegetable oil. Then mix all ingredients thoroughly. Bake at 350° for 35 to 40 minutes.

BAKED RICE

Serves 4

1 C. uncooked rice
3 C. canned, less salt, chicken broth
3 T. no salt margarine

Brown rice in margarine in skillet. Add chicken broth and bring to a boil. Turn down heat to simmer, cover and bake at 350° for 50 minutes or until rice is tender.

COPPER PENNIES

Serves 6

2 lbs. carrots, peeled and sliced
1-10 oz. can low salt tomato soup
1 T. Worcestershire sauce
1 white onion, sliced
¾ C. salad oil
1 tsp. prepared mustard
1 green pepper, sliced
¾ C. vinegar
Pepper to taste

With knife, prepare vegetables. Cook carrots until tender. Drain. Put all other ingredients together and bring to a boil. Remove from heat and add carrots. Store in refrigerator for 24 hours before serving. Can be served hot or cold. Don't worry about leftovers as this can be stored in refrigerator for 3 weeks.

BAKED CORN

Serves 4

2 C. canned corn (no salt added)
1 T. no salt margarine
½ C. skim milk
2 egg whites, well beaten
2 tsp. flour
1 tsp. black pepper

Combine all ingredients; mix thoroughly. Pour into non-stick pan or spray pan with vegetable spray. Bake at 400° until inserted knife comes out clean.

QUICK ASPARAGUS CASSEROLE

Serves 4

1 large can no salt asparagus
1 can no salt cream of mushroom soup
4 to 6 slices lowfat mozzarella cheese

Drain asparagus. In non-stick 8" baking dish or spray dish with vegetable spray place asparagus. Cover with soup. Place cheese on top and bake until cheese melts well.

CREOLE CELERY DELIGHT

Serves 4

2 T. no salt margarine
½ C. green pepper, chopped
2 C. cooked tomatoes (may be fresh or canned; no salt added if canned)
½ C. white onions, chopped
2 C. diced celery
Season with garlic salt (optional)

Prepare, cutting vegetables with knife. Saute onion and green pepper in margarine until golden brown. Add tomatoes, celery and garlic salt which is optional. Simmer on low heat until tender. Do not overcook.

PEAS & CELERY   Serves 4

½ C. celery, chopped
½ tsp. thyme leaves
1-10 oz. pkg. frozen peas
1 T. no salt margarine, melted

In saucepan over medium heat cook celery in ⅔ cup water about 7 minutes. Add peas and cook 8 to 10 minutes. Drain. Sprinkle with thyme; toss with no salt margarine.

LOW CAL GREEN BEANS

Serves 4

1-10 oz. pkg. frozen French-
style green beans
2½ tsp. vegetable oil

¼ tsp. black pepper
2 tsp. white wine vinegar

Cook green beans as directed. Drain. In small skillet in vegetable oil saute beans until they just begin to brown. Season to taste with vinegar and pepper.

BAKED GREEN PEPPERS

Serves 4

4 green peppers
½ clove garlic, chopped
2 T. olive oil

With knife, cut peppers into quarters; remove stems, membranes and seeds. Mix peppers, garlic and olive oil in pan. Bake uncovered at 325° for 20 to 25 minutes, stirring frequently.

BRUSSELS SPROUTS & MUSHROOMS

Serves 4

1½ lbs. Brussels sprout
1 white onion, chopped
1 T. lemon juice
3 T. no salt margarine
½ lb. mushrooms, sliced
1/8 tsp. garlic powder

Soak sprouts for 5 minutes in cold water. Rinse and drain. Place sprouts into boiling water; lower heat and simmer 12 minutes. Remove from heat and drain. With knife, slice onions and mushrooms. In small skillet melt margarine. Saute mushrooms and onions 5 minutes. Add lemon juice, garlic powder and sprouts. Mix thoroughly.

SAUTEED ZUCCHINI STRIPS

Serves 4

4 small zucchini
4 T. vegetable oil
¼ tsp. black pepper
½ tsp. oregano
1 clove garlic, finely chopped

Wash the zucchini, but do not peel. With a knife, cut into strips ⅓" wide by 2½" long. Heat vegetable oil in skillet; saute zucchini strips on low heat until browned on all sides. Add pepper, oregano and garlic. Cook an additional 5 minutes on low heat.

PINEAPPLE CARROTS

Serves 4

1-8 oz. can crushed
   pineapple, drained
½ C. water

2 C. carrots, sliced and diced
1 tsp. cornstarch

With a knife, prepare carrots. In pan combine drained crushed pineapple and water. Add carrots. Cover and cook on low simmer 15 to 20 minutes. Add cornstarch and 2 tablespoons of water to carrots. Cook and stir over low heat till it bubbles. Season with pepper to taste.

GREEN BEANS IN MUSTARD SAUCE

Serves 4

1 can no salt added green beans, drained
1 T. flour
1 T. Worcestershire sauce
1 T. no salt margarine
¾ C. skim milk
4 T. prepared mild yellow mustard

Cook beans as directed and keep warm. Melt margarine over low heat and blend in flour. Add ¾ cup skim milk and heat, stirring constantly, until thickened. Mix in remaining ingredients and heat, stirring 5 minutes. Pour mustard mixture over beans. Toss lightly to mix. Pepper to taste.

QUICK BROILED ZUCCHINI WITH CHEESE — Serves 4

4 zucchini
4 oz. shredded lowfat
  mozzarella cheese

Salad oil
Garlic salt
Black pepper

With knife, cut zucchini lengthwise in half. Set oven control at broiler or 550°. Place zucchini cut sides up in pan. Brush with salad oil and sprinkle with garlic salt and black pepper to taste. Top with lowfat mozzarella cheese.

CABBAGE SALAD

Serves 4

3 C. shredded cabbage
1 C. sliced apples
½ C. celery
1 C. sliced pineapple
1 C. miniature marshmallows
1 C. plain lowfat yogurt

Mix all together except yogurt. Chill. Mix in chilled yogurt just before serving. Be sure to mix yogurt in well.

SPINACH

Serves 4

2 lbs. spinach, washed well
1 large white onion, cut
   in half

3 T. vegetable oil

With a knife, prepare spinach and onion. Cut off root ends and wash spinach well. Drain. Cut onion in half. Place vegetable oil in saucepan. Place onion halves cut sides down in oil and place spinach leaves on onion. Cover and cook until water has evaporated or about 5 to 10 minutes.

STEWED TOMATOES

Serves 4

4 tomatoes (about 1½ lbs.), peeled and cut into pieces
⅔ C. white onion, finely chopped
1 bay leaf
Ground pepper
½ C. chopped green pepper
1 C. whole wheat bread crumbs

With a knife, prepare tomatoes, onion and pepper. Mix tomatoes, onion, green pepper and bay leaf in pan. Heat to boiling, stirring occasionally. Cover. On low heat simmer 9 to 11 minutes. Stir in whole wheat bread crumbs and heat. Remove bay leaf and season to taste with pepper.

SALADS

YOGURT & FRUIT SALAD

Serves 6

1 can mandarin oranges
1 can pineapple tidbits
1 can fruit cocktail
1 C. diced apples
⅓ C. pecans
1 C. marshmallows
1 C. plain lowfat yogurt

All cans of fruit should be bought in water or in its own juices, no sugar added. Drain cans of fruit. Mix all ingredients together and chill.

CAULIFLOWER SALAD

Serves 4

1 head cauliflower, cut and broken into small pieces
4 oz. light cream cheese, softened
3 grated carrots
1 C. plain lowfat yogurt
2 T. diced onions
⅓ C. shredded mozzarella cheese (made with skim milk)

Mix together the yogurt and cream cheese. Mix together all remaining ingredients until mixed well. Chill for 1 to 2 hours.

GREEN SALAD

Serves 6

- 1 can no salt added green beans, drained
- 1 can no salt added wax beans, drained
- 4 C. celery, finely sliced
- 2 T. water
- 1 can no salt added green peas, drained
- 1 can kidney beans, drained
- 1 C. vinegar
- ½ C. oil

Mix all ingredients together. Toss lightly and marinate overnight.

REFRESHING YOGURT COLESLAW

Serves 4

4 C. cabbage, shredded fine	1 C. plain lowfat yogurt
	1½ T. white vinegar
	2 tsp. caraway seed
¼ tsp. low sodium salt	1/8 tsp. black pepper

Chill cabbage. Combine remaining ingredients; cover and chill. Toss dressing and cabbage just before serving.

CUCUMBER SALAD

Serves 4

1 lb. cucumbers
1 tsp. vegetable oil
1/8 tsp. MSG

1 T. lite soy sauce
1 tsp. white vinegar
1 tsp. sherry

Combine soy sauce, sherry, oil and monosodium glutamate (MSG) for the dressing. Peel and halve the cucumbers; remove seeds and cut into thin slices. Add dressing and chill.

COLD BROCCOLI SALAD

Serves 8

8 oz. shredded mozzarella cheese (made with skim milk)
2 C. plain lowfat yogurt
½ C. white vinegar
2 heads broccoli, cut up
2 white onions, chopped
½ C. vegetable oil

Prepare all ingredients. Combine cheese, onion, yogurt, oil and vinegar. Toss with cut up broccoli. Makes about 8 cups. Refrigerate any leftovers.

5-CUP SALAD

Serves 4

1 C. pineapple tidbits, drained
1 C. miniature marshmallows
1 C. chopped pecans
1 C. mandarin oranges
1 C. plain lowfat yogurt
Maraschino cherries to garnish, optional

Mix all ingredients. Chill overnight.

PEA SALAD

Serves 4

1 head lettuce
1 cucumber, sliced thin
1-10 oz. pkg. frozen peas
¾ C. white onion, chopped
½ C. green pepper, diced
12 oz. shredded mozzarella cheese (made with skim milk)
1½ C. plain lowfat yogurt

Layer 1 head lettuce in glass dish (13x9"). Mix together onion, cucumber, green pepper and peas and spread on layered lettuce. Spread 1½ cups plain lowfat yogurt over ingredients and cover with mozzarella cheese.

CHINESE SALAD

Serves 4

- 1 can no salt Chinese mixed vegetables
- 1 can water chestnuts
- 1 small jar pimentos
- ¾ C. white vinegar
- 1 can no salt mixed vegetables
- 1¼ C. celery
- 2 green onions, chopped
- ½ C. vegetable oil

Mix oil and vinegar and pour over vegetables. Marinate overnight. Leftovers are great as this dish keeps well for several days.

LIGHT FRUIT SALAD

Serves 6

1 can lite peaches
1 can mandarin oranges, drained
1 pkg. NutraSweet vanilla instant pudding
1 can pineapple tidbits, drained
1-10 oz. pkg. frozen strawberries
5 golden ripe bananas

Drain and combine peaches, pineapple and oranges. Stir in NutraSweet instant pudding. (Add a little fruit juice or water if the pudding does not mix well.) Thaw strawberries and add them to the mixture. Add 5 bananas, sliced.

MARINATED FRUIT SALAD

Serves 6

2 CUPS OF THE FOLLOWING FRUITS:

Raw apples
Pineapple chunks
Strawberries (fresh)
Golden ripe bananas
Seedless grapes
Oranges (fresh)
Pears (fresh)

Combine all fruits except strawberries in large bowl and pour 1 can thawed orange juice over them. Marinate overnight and top with fresh strawberries when you serve.

SEVEN LAYER SALAD

Serves 6

1 large head lettuce, torn in pieces
2 green peppers, chopped
1-10 oz. pkg. frozen peas
8 oz. shredded mozzarella cheese (made with skim milk)
2 white onions, chopped
4 celery stalks, chopped
1 C. plain lowfat yogurt

Place bed of lettuce in bottom of dish. Layer in other ingredients. Spread lowfat yogurt on top of peas. Sprinkle with mozzarella cheese. Refrigerate overnight and serve.

CARROT-RAISIN SALAD

Serves 4

2½ C. grated carrots
½ C. lowfat plain yogurt
½ C. seedless raisins
1 T. lemon juice

Combine carrots and raisins and set aside. Mix together yogurt and lemon juice. Stir sauce into carrot-raisin mixture. Chill. Serve on lettuce.

RICE SALAD

Serves 4 to 6

2½ C. long grain brown rice
1 T. fresh ginger, finely minced
2 carrots, grated
1 C. plain lowfat yogurt
¼ tsp. cinnamon
½ C. seedless raisins

Combine all ingredients in a bowl and mix well. Refrigerate overnight. Serve on lettuce leaves.

ZUCCHINI-MUSHROOM SALAD

Serves 6

2 medium-size zucchini, thinly sliced
2 medium tomatoes, chopped
3 T. vegetable salad oil
½ tsp. ground pepper
2 C. fresh sliced mushrooms
¼ C. chopped white onions
3 T. white vinegar

In bowl mix mushrooms, zucchini slices, tomatoes and onion.
DRESSING: Mix well vegetable salad oil, vinegar and ground pepper.
Toss dressing with vegetables and refrigerate overnight.

RED CABBAGE-APPLE SLAW

Serves 6

1 small head red cabbage, cored
3 large unpeeled apples, cored
¼ C. plain lowfat yogurt
¼ C. apple cider vinegar

Use a food processor or grater to finely shred the cabbage and apples. Place in large bowl and stir in vinegar and yogurt. Stir well. Refrigerate overnight. Stir once before serving.

SPINACH SALAD

Serves 6

6 C. torn spinach leaves
2 green peppers, cut into small strips
½ C. shredded mozzarella cheese (made with skim milk)
⅓ C. white vinegar
½ C. sliced radishes
1¼ C. shredded carrots
⅓ C. vegetable salad oil

In bowl combine spinach, radishes, green peppers, shredded carrots and shredded mozzarella cheese. Toss to mix. Mix white vinegar and salad oil for dressing. Pour dressing over salad.

ASPARAGUS-YOGURT SALAD

Serves 6

1½ lbs. fresh asparagus
1 clove garlic, crushed
1 T. chopped fresh parsley
1 C. plain lowfat yogurt
⅓ tsp. Worcestershire sauce
1 head lettuce, cored and torn into leaves

With a knife, remove ends of asparagus and scales from stalks. Cook asparagus covered in small amount of boiling water 6 to 8 minutes or until tender; drain and chill asparagus. Combine yogurt, parsley, garlic and Worcestershire sauce; cover and chill for 2 hours. Serve asparagus on lettuce leaves; top with yogurt mixture.

QUICK POTATO SALAD

Serves 4

4 potatoes, peeled and quartered
2 T. vinegar
1 T. vegetable oil
1 tsp. dry mustard
1 bay leaf
½ C. boiling water
½ C. plain lowfat yogurt
1 small white onion, chopped
¾ tsp. onion powder

In large pan add potatoes, bay leaf and onion powder. (Make sure you use enough water to cover potatoes in pan.) Cook potatoes 25 to 30 minutes or until tender. Drain. When cool enough to handle, peel and slice into a bowl. Combine vinegar, boiling water and oil. Pour over potatoes and toss well. Cool. Combine yogurt (do not use mayonnaise) and a touch of garlic powder with potatoes.

STUFFED TOMATO SALAD

Serves 6

6 large red ripe tomatoes
1 can water-packed lite tuna, drained
2 tsp. parsley
¼ C. plain lowfat yogurt
2 small white onions, minced
Black pepper to taste
1 C. cooked rice

Cut top off tomatoes. Scoop out pulp and place in bowl. To pulp add remaining ingredients except cooked rice. Mash thoroughly. Add rice and blend well. Stuff tomatoes with rice mixture.

CRANBERRY SALAD

Serves 10

- 2 small pkgs. sugar-free raspberry jello
- 1 C. whole cranberry sauce
- 3 large apples, diced small
- ½ C. chopped pecans, optional
- 1½ C. hot water
- 1-16 oz. can crushed pineapple
- ½ C. celery, diced

Dissolve jello in hot water. Add cranberries and stir until smooth, except for berries. Add pineapple, apples, celery and pecans (optional). Stir until mixed. Refrigerate.

SUMMER SALAD

Serves 6

1 head broccoli, cut in pieces
1 head cauliflower, cut in pieces
1 white onion, diced fine
1 C. shredded mozzarella cheese (made with skim milk)
½ C. sour cream
1 green pepper, diced
1 C. plain lowfat yogurt

Mix cream cheese and yogurt. Pour over vegetables and cheese. Do not stir. Refrigerate overnight. Stir once before serving.

CORN SALAD

Serves 4

- 1 can no salt whole kernel corn, drained
- 1 C. finely chopped celery
- 3 tsp. prepared mustard
- 3 T. salad oil
- 1 C. chopped green pepper
- 1 C. white onions, chopped
- ¼ C. chopped pimento
- ¼ C. vinegar

With a knife, prepare items. Combine all ingredients. Chill and serve.

FISH/SEAFOOD

EASY CAMPER FISH DINNER

Serves 6

6 large fish fillets
6 pats or tsp. low salt margarine
1½ C. barbecue sauce
6 white onion slices

Stack one of each ingredient in piece of foil large enough to wrap and seal. Pepper to taste. Wrap and place on grill for 20 to 25 minutes.

ASPARAGUS FILET OF SOLE

Serves 4

- 4 large sole filets
- 1 lb. asparagus spears
- 3 T. melted low salt margarine
- 2 T. lemon juice
- 2 tsp. Dijon mustard

With your knife, cut asparagus spears into 2 to 3" lengths. Cook in boiling water 5 minutes; drain. In vegetable spray baking dish place asparagus spears at one end of each filet. Roll up filet with spears inside and secure with foodpicks. Combine remaining ingredients; pour over fish. Bake at 425° for 15 minutes or until fish flakes easily.

MOZZARELLA FISH DELITE

Serves 4

1½ lbs. fish fillets (perch, cod or sole)
¾ C. whole wheat bread crumbs
8 oz. thinly sliced lowfat mozzarella cheese
1-8 oz. can no salt tomato sauce
¼ tsp. garlic salt

In non-stick baking pan or spray with vegetable oil arrange fillets. Thinly spread tomato sauce over fish. Sprinkle garlic salt and bread crumbs over fish. Top with thin slices lowfat mozzarella cheese. Bake at 375° for 10 minutes or until cheese bubbles. If you would prefer fillets to be golden brown, place under broiler for couple of minutes.

LIGHT TUNA CHEF SALAD

Serves 6

- 2 cans lite water-packed tuna, drained
- 1 white onion, sliced
- 8 C. torn lettuce
- ¾ C. wine vinegar
- 1 cucumber, sliced
- 2 tsp. dried basil leaves, crushed
- 1½ C. cherry tomatoes, halved
- ½ C. diced celery
- 2 tsp. sugar substitute

Mix vinegar, sugar substitute and basil leaves. Chill. Toss remaining ingredients together. Pour chilled dressing over and toss lightly.

TUNA TACOS

Serves 6

12 taco shells
4 T. chopped white onion
2 C. fresh chopped tomatoes
Taco sauce (optional)
2 cans lite water-packed tuna, drained

1/8 tsp. garlic powder
2 C. shredded lettuce
1 C. chopped celery
⅓ C. low cal French dressing
8 oz. low cal mozzarella cheese, shredded

In bowl mix tuna, celery, onion and garlic powder. Stir in low cal dressing. Spoon mixture in taco shells; top with tomato, mozzarella cheese and lettuce. (Pass optional taco sauce.)

WISCONSIN LAKE TROUT MOZZARELLA AU GRATIN

Serves 4

4 lbs. fish, about 4 lake trout cleaned
3 T. low salt margarine, melted
½ C. lowfat mozzarella cheese, shredded
Juice of 1 lemon
8 oz. white sauce (made with skim milk)
2 egg whites, beaten

Cut fish into serving portions and season with lemon juice. Pepper to taste and add low salt margarine; cover and bake 20 minutes. Whip egg whites and add to white sauce; add ½ of mozzarella cheese. Mask fish with this sauce; sprinkle with remaining cheese and dot with melted butter. Bake until browned.

BAKED MOZZARELLA BASS

Serves 6

5 lbs. fish, about 6
bass cleaned
1 T. flour
½ C. corn meal

8 oz. sliced mozzarella cheese
(made with skim milk)
1 tsp. black pepper
2 white onions, optional

Mix flour, corn meal and pepper to taste. Dip fish in corn meal mixture. Place in non-stick baking dish or spray with vegetable oil. Top with mozzarella cheese. Bake at 400° for 20 minutes or until cheese is well melted. (Optional: Onions may be baked around the fish thinly sliced.)

TOMATO BAKED SHRIMP

Serves 4

2 lbs. frozen shelled shrimp
¼ tsp. garlic powder

1 can low sodium tomato soup
2-4 oz. cans mushrooms, drained
3 tsp. parsley flakes

Cook shrimp as package directs. In medium pan combine undiluted tomato soup and remaining ingredients. Heat to boiling; add shrimp to sauce.
(Shrimp are high in cholesterol and this recipe should be used only as a special treat for shrimp lovers.)

BAKED CARP

Serves 6

4 lbs. carp
1 C. celery, chopped
½ C. low salt margarine
2 white onions, sliced

1 C. no salt, canned or fresh tomatoes
2 carrots, chopped
2 green peppers, chopped
⅓ C. flour

In non-stick baking dish or spray with vegetable oil (9x13x2") dish, place all chopped vegetables on bottom. Flour carp; place carp on top of vegetables. Pepper to taste. Lightly drizzle melted margarine over carp. Bake at 375° for 40 to 45 minutes; baste with its own juice every 15 minutes.

BAKED HALIBUT

Serves 4

4 halibut steaks
⅓ C. skim milk

5 T. melted low salt margarine
2 C. cornflakes, crushed

Dip steaks in low salt margarine, then in the crushed cornflakes to coat on both sides. Place on non-stick baking sheet or spray with vegetable oil. Pour melted margarine over steaks. Bake at 500° for 15 to 20 minutes.

WINO TROUT

Serves 4

6 trout (6 to 8 oz. each)
½ C. dry white wine
4 tsp. lemon juice
½ C. low salt margarine
White pepper

Brush inside of fish with pepper and melted margarine. Brush outside with lemon juice and white pepper. Pour wine around fish. Cover and bake at 375° for 15 to 20 minutes or until flaky.

BAKED SOLE WITH MUSHROOMS

Serves 4

1 onion, chopped	Salt and pepper to taste
2 T. chopped parsley	¼ C. dry white wine
1 C. sliced mushrooms	½ C. skim milk
¼ C. low salt margarine	1 T. flour
8 sole fillets, about 1¼ lbs.	Paprika

Preheat oven to 350°. Saute onion, parsley and mushrooms in 3 tablespoons of the margarine, stirring until onions are tender. Place 4 fillets in a greased baking dish. Sprinkle lightly with salt and pepper and spread sauteed mixture over fish. Top with remaining fillets, pour wine over all and dot with remaining margarine. Bake uncovered for 15 minutes. Remove from oven and drain, reserve pan liquid. In a small saucepan combine flour and milk. Add the reserved pan liquid and cook, stirring until thickened. Pour over fish and bake 5 minutes longer. Sprinkle with paprika and parsley.

MARINADE GRILLED SWORDFISH

Serves 4

4 swordfish steaks

MARINADE:
Juice of 4 limes
1½ oz. tequila
2 tsp. olive oil
Dash of cayenne pepper

Mix marinade in medium-size bowl. Marinate steaks all day or overnight in refrigerator. Broil steaks 6 to 7 minutes on each side. Baste occasionally with any remaining marinade mixture during cooking.

OVEN-POACHED HADDOCK

Serves 6

3 lbs. haddock fillets
1 bay leaf
Juice of 2 lemons
½ tsp. thyme

3 T. white onion, finely chopped
4 fresh tomatoes, sliced
Black pepper

Cut fillets into 6 servings and place in non-stick baking dish or spray dish with vegetable oil. Mix lemon juice, onions, bay leaf and thyme; spoon onto fillets. Cover and refrigerate 2 to 3 hours. Bake at 350°. Arrange tomato slices on fillets and season with pepper to taste. Cover and bake 45 to 50 minutes or until fish flakes easily.

ORANGE RUFFIE FISH FILLETS WITH PINEAPPLE

Serves 4

1 1/2 lbs. orange ruffie fillets	2 white onions
1 T. sugar substitute	2 T. cornstarch
1 tsp. ground ginger	1 T. lite soy sauce
2 C. pineapple pieces in its own juice	2 T. vegetable oil
	1/4 C. lemon juice

Using knife, cut fish into serving size pieces. Place in 3-quart casserole dish. Slice onions and saute in hot vegetable oil in pan. Mix all other ingredients and pour into pan, stirring until mixture thickens. Pour sauce over fish in casserole. Cover and bake at 350° for 30 to 35 minutes. Serve with rice.

TUNA CHOPSTICK DELITE

Serves 4

- 2 cans low sodium cream of mushroom soup
- ½ C. white onion, chopped
- 1 C. celery
- ½ C. water
- 4 C. Chinese noodles (thin)
- 2 cans lite water-packed tuna, drained

In non-stick baking dish or spray with vegetable oil combine all ingredients. Bake for 55 to 60 minutes and pepper to taste.

QUICK BROILED FISH

Serves 4

1½ lbs. fresh fish fillets
3 T. low salt margarine
3 tsp. lemon juice

Mix margarine and lemon juice in small pan over low heat. Brush a broiler pan with mixture. Place fish on broiler pan. Brush remaining mixture on fish. Broil about 10 minutes turning once.

FILLET OF SOLE

Serves 4

1½ lbs. (6 to 8 fillets) of sole
4 T. unsalted margarine
⅓ C. flour
4 tsp. lemon juice
¼ tsp. white pepper

Dip fillets in mixture of flour and pepper. Melt half the margarine in a skillet. Cook fillets until browned on both sides. Take out fillets and transfer to platter. Clean skillet. Melt the remaining margarine in the skillet until it turns brown in color. Add lemon juice and pour over the fish.

RED SNAPPER FILLET

Serves 6

6 red snapper fillets,
6 to 8 oz. each
1½ C. mild chili salsa

3 T. olive oil
1½ tsp. chili powder

Over medium heat coat skillet with olive oil. Add snapper fillets. Fry briefly and add remaining ingredients. Cover and cook on low heat 15 minutes or until flaky. (Optional: Garnish with lemon wedges.)

LOW CAL TUNA SALAD

Serves 6

2 cans lite water-packed tuna, drained
1/3 tsp. ground pepper
3 tsp. lemon juice
1/4 C. plain lowfat yogurt

Mix with tuna all ingredients. Serve on lettuce leaves. (Optional: Whole wheat bread.)

BAKED SALMON STEAKS

Serves 2

½ lb. fresh salmon steaks
4 mushrooms, chopped
1 T. chopped onion
1 tsp. minced parsley
2 tsp. unsalted butter
1 oz. sherry
1 T. fine bread crumbs

In a shallow baking dish place the salmon. Sprinkle salmon with mushrooms, onion and parsley. Dot with butter. Add sherry and bake in a 350° oven for 15 minutes. Then sprinkle with the crumbs and continue baking another 15 minutes, basting several times.

HOLLY MACKEREL WITH YOGURT & CHIVES   Serves 4

1½ lbs. mackerel fillets, cut into 4 servings
⅓ C. polyunsaturated oil
4 T. flour
1½ C. plain lowfat yogurt
¼ C. snipped chives

Coat mackerel fillets with flour and fry on each side until browned. Drain oil. Pour the mixed yogurt and chives over fillets.

TURBOT ITALIANO

Serves 4

1½ lbs. turbot fillets
8 oz. shredded mozzarella cheese (made with skim milk)
½ C. no salt tomato sauce
1½ tsp. garlic salt

In a non-stick dish or spray with vegetable oil bake fillets for 30 to 35 minutes at 350°. Put no salt tomato sauce over fish and bake another 10 minutes. Sprinkle with garlic salt and top with shredded lowfat mozzarella cheese. Return to oven just long enough for cheese to melt.

CALIFORNIA SCALLOPS

Serves 4

- 1½ lbs. scallops
- 2 medium-size tomatoes, halved
- 1 T. no salt margarine, melted
- 1 T. vegetable oil
- ½ tsp. black pepper
- 1 garlic clove, chopped
- 2 T. lemon juice

Let scallops stand in oil and garlic for 15 to 20 minutes. Sprinkle tomato halves with pepper. Place scallops in pan. Over scallops pour melted margarine. Broil about 10 minutes, turning scallops once.

CRAB BISQUE

Serves 6

2-8 oz. cans king crab, drained	½ tsp. pepper
1 C. skimmed milk	1 can low salt condensed tomato soup
3 T. no salt margarine	3 T. minced onions
	½ tsp. low sodium salt

In medium saucepan, cook onion and margarine till tender. Add remaining ingredients but crab; cook on low heat for 5 minutes. Add crab and cook 15 minutes on medium heat. Do not boil. Refrigerate any leftovers.

TANGY FISH

Serves 4

1½ lbs. fish fillets
2 T. minced onion

1½ C. no salt tomato juice
¼ tsp. black pepper
½ C. mustard

Place fish fillets in non-stick casserole dish or spray with vegetable oil. Mix together remaining ingredients and pour over fish. Bake 25 to 30 minutes at 350°.

BAKED TUNA FISH CAKES

Serves 4

2 cans lite water-packed tuna, drained
1 C. no salt tomato juice
3 T. Worcestershire sauce
¼ C. white onions, chopped finely
4 T. chopped celery
4 tsp. prepared mustard

Combine all ingredients and form into patties. In a non-stick pan or spray with Pam vegetable oil, bake at 350° for 30 to 35 minutes. Pepper to taste.

MUSHROOM BAKED SOLE

Serves 4

1 onion, chopped	8 sole fillets (about 1¼ lbs.)
2 T. chopped parsley	¼ C. dry white wine
1 C. sliced mushrooms	½ C. skim milk
¼ C. unsalted margarine	1 T. flour

Preheat oven to 350°. Saute onion, parsley and mushrooms in 3 tablespoons of the margarine, stirring until onions are tender. Place 4 fillets in a greased baking dish. Sprinkle lightly with salt and pepper and spread sauteed mixture over fish. Top with remaining 4 fillets. Pour wine over all and dot with remaining margarine. Bake uncovered for 15 minutes. Remove from oven and drain, reserving the pan liquid. In a small saucepan, combine flour and milk. Add the reserved pan liquid and cook, stirring until thickened. Pour over the fish and bake 5 minutes longer. Sprinkle with paprika and parsley.

CRAB "STUFFED" FLOUNDER

Serves 6

1 lb. crabmeat	4 T. plain lowfat yogurt
2 tsp. instant minced onion	¼ tsp. cayenne pepper
1 ½ C. whole wheat bread crumbs	2 lbs. flounder fillets
	1 tsp. dry mustard

Mix crabmeat, yogurt, onions, mustard, cayenne pepper and 1 cup of whole wheat bread crumbs. Spread mixture in a non-stick pan or spray with vegetable oil; spread mixture so that the bottom of the pan is well covered. Place flounder fillets on top. Sprinkle the flounder with remaining bread crumbs. Bake, uncovered, 475° for 30 minutes or until flounder is tender.

ITALIAN FISH STEAKS

Serves 4

1½ lbs. halibut, shark or other firm whitefish

1½ C. no salt Italian marinara sauce
8 oz. lowfat shredded mozzarella cheese

Place steaks in non-stick casserole pan or spray with vegetable oil. Cover fish with sauce. Broil for 15 minutes, turning once to cook each side. Spoon sauce over fish after turning. Remove from broiler and sprinkle with mozzarella cheese. Return to oven and broil until cheese is melted and slightly browned.

BARBECUED HERBED FISH

Serves 6

2 lbs. fish (whitefish or fresh water fish)	Fresh dill or other leafy herbs
1 tsp. pepper	½ C. no salt margarine
2 T. lemon juice	1 tsp. coriander seed, crushed
	1 C. plain lowfat yogurt

Melt no salt margarine. Mix in seasonings, lemon juice and yogurt. Coat fish inside and out with mixture. Place in wire broil basket and cook over coals till fish browns on both sides, about 30 minutes. Brush often with sauce mixture. Ten minutes before end of cooking time, make bed of leafy herbs on grill top. Lay fish on top. Grill till herbs smolder and flavor the fish. Turn once.

SOUPS

APPETIZER SOUP
Serves 4

1⅓ C. water
2 beef bouillon cubes
1 tsp. lemon juice
1½ tsp. horseradish
¼ tsp. dill weed
5 lemon slices

Mix and heat all ingredients, except lemon, to boiling. Serve hot and garnish with lemon slices.

ZUCCHINI SOUP

Serves 6

6 zucchini, sliced
2-11 oz. cans, less salt, clear chicken broth
½ tsp. lite soy sauce
1 C. plain lowfat yogurt
1 C. white onions, chopped
1 tsp. curry powder
¾ C. long grain rice
1 C. water
2 tsp. Dijon mustard

In large pan, combine zucchini, chopped onion, long grain rice, water, chicken broth, soy sauce. (If necessary, add more water to cover zucchini.) Slowly simmer for 20 to 25 minutes or until zucchini is tender. Mix in blender, adding curry powder, yogurt and mustard. May serve warm or cool. Leftovers; no worry as this soup freezes well.

BOUILLABAISSE SOUP

Serves 6

3 T. vegetable oil	2 white onions, chopped
1 green pepper, finely chopped	4-8 oz. cans no salt tomato sauce
2 C. water	10 scallops
8 oysters	1¼ C. chopped celery
8 shrimp pieces	Crab chunks

Heat oil in a large kettle. Saute onion, celery and pepper. Add no salt tomato sauce and water. Simmer for 25 minutes. Add the seafood items, one kind at a time. When all have been added, cook until seafood is done, about 10 minutes. Do not overcook. Don't worry about leftovers as this soup freezes well.

FARMERS STEW

Serves 6

2 lbs. ground turkey
1 can no salt whole kernel corn
1 large can no salt tomatoes, chopped
1 white onion, chopped
1 T. chili powder
1 large potato, cut in small pieces
2 green peppers, chopped
3 carrots, chopped
½ C. celery, chopped

Simmer vegetables in large saucepan until done. Brown turkey in skillet. Drain off any fat. Add vegetables and chili powder. Pepper to taste.

FISH CREOLE

Serves 6

- 3 lbs. skinless, boneless fish, such as striped bass, red snapper or blackfish
- 2 T. + 1 tsp. vegetable oil
- 1 large onion, chopped
- 2 tsp. finely chopped garlic
- 1 C. chopped celery
- 2 C. chopped green pepper
- 2 C. peeled, cored tomatoes, cubed
- 1 bay leaf
- ½ tsp. dried thyme
- Pepper to taste

Preheat oven to 425°. Cut each fillet into 3 pieces of equal size. Heat 2 tablespoons oil in a skillet and add the onion. Cook until tender and add garlic, celery and cook about 2 minutes stirring. Add the green pepper. Cook, stirring about 5 minutes. Add the tomatoes, bay leaf and thyme. Cook for about 10 minutes. Rub 1 teaspoon of oil in a baking dish. Arrange the fish in one layer. Sprinkle with pepper. Spoon the Creole sauce over all. Cover and bake 20 minutes. Uncover and bake 10 minutes longer.

HOMEMADE CHICKEN STOCK

4 to 8 boneless and skinned chicken breasts, cut into pieces
3 carrots, sliced
1-11 oz. can, less salt, clear chicken broth
1 stalk celery, sliced
1 white onion, sliced
¼ tsp. thyme

In large pan, mix together all ingredients; cover with water and bring to a boil for 5 minutes. Cover pan with lid; reduce heat and simmer for 1¾ hours. Remove chicken and vegetables. Refrigerate stock in kettle overnight. Next day, skim off any excess fat. Separate and freeze any extra in storage containers.

MUSHROOM SOUP

Serves 4

1 lb. fresh mushrooms, sliced
2-11 oz. cans, less salt, clear chicken broth
¼ C. lemon juice (or may use juice of 1 large lemon)
1 T. dry vermouth
2½ T. no salt margarine
1 T. dry sherry

In small pan, saute fresh mushrooms in no salt margarine until tender. Mix together with chicken broth and remaining ingredients.

BROCCOLI SOUP

Serves 6

1 C. diced white onions
½ C. celery
¼ tsp. cayenne pepper
2 C. skim milk
3 T. no salt margarine
2 C. water
½ C. long grain rice
½ tsp. low sodium salt, optional

4 to 6 cups of broccoli (suit to taste). 6 cups will take 2 fresh heads of broccoli. You may also use frozen broccoli.

In a small pan, saute onion and celery in margarine until tender. Mix in water, low sodium salt (optional), cayenne pepper and long grain rice. Cover pan with lid and simmer for about 15 minutes. Meanwhile, steam cook broccoli until it is tender. Mix chopped up broccoli into soup and continue cooking for at least 15 minutes or until the broccoli is soft and rice is cooked.

CUCUMBER SOUP

Serves 4

3 cucumbers
1-11 oz. can, less salt, clear chicken broth
3 C. plain lowfat yogurt
1 clove garlic, chopped
¾ T. olive oil

With knife, peel and slice cucumbers into bite-size pieces and set aside (do not salt). Mix 3 cups lowfat yogurt into a medium-size pan and stir until smooth. Stir in chicken broth (you may want to add ¼ cup of water if mixture is too thick). Mix in garlic and olive oil. Add cucumbers to yogurt mixture. Chill in refrigerator for 4 to 6 hours.

FISH CHOWDER

Serves 6

4 C. water
¼ C. chopped parsley
1 small bay leaf
½ tsp. dried thyme
½ tsp. salt
Pepper to taste
½ tsp. dried orange peel
2 fennel seeds
1 lb. haddock, halibut, snapper or other fish, boned
1 medium onion, chopped
1 C. chopped celery
2 large potatoes, sliced thin
2 C. skim milk

In a large saucepan, combine first 8 ingredients and bring to a boil. Add the boned fish and simmer 15 minutes. Remove fish from the broth and cut into small pieces. Add the onion, celery and potatoes to the broth and simmer until potatoes are tender. Add the skim milk, heat to simmer and add the fish. Heat through.

CABBAGE SOUP

Serves 6

½ cabbage

6 C. less salt, canned chicken broth

With knife, slice into pieces ½ cabbage. Add chicken stock to cabbage and simmer until cooked. Pepper to taste.

CARROT SOUP

Serves 6

3 T. no salt margarine
2 large potatoes, peeled and chopped
2 lbs. carrots
1 bay leaf
2 white onions, sliced
7 C. clear, less salt, chicken broth

With knife, slice onions, carrots and potatoes. Melt margarine in large pan on low heat. Add carrots and onions. Cover with a circle of waxed paper and let sweat about 6 minutes. Remove waxed paper. Add potatoes, bay leaf, chicken stock and cover. Simmer until vegetables are tender, about 45 minutes. Puree soup. Return to pan and season with pepper to taste. Place on medium heat. Bring to boil, stirring occasionally.

POTATO & LEEK SOUP

Serves 4

4 C. leeks, washed and sliced
Clear, less salt, chicken broth
4 C. potateos, peeled and cubed
½ C. skim milk
1 tsp. thyme

With knife, prepare vegetables. Put vegetables in a large pan and add sufficient chicken stock to cover. Cook vegetables until tender, about 35 minutes. Put through food processor and return to pot. Add skim milk and season with thyme. Heat through and serve hot.

FRESH TOMATO SOUP

Serves 6

3 medium-size white onions, chopped
1½ C. clear, less salt, chicken broth
5 large ripe tomatoes, cored peeled and quartered
2 T. no salt margarine
1 stalk celery, cut in 1" pieces
¼ tsp. pepper

Mix onions, celery and chicken broth in a large pan; cover and slowly simmer for 50 minutes or until onions are mushy. Add fresh tomatoes; cover and simmer 20 minutes or until tomatoes have reduced to juice. Cool 15 minutes then puree in blender for 20 seconds. Return to pan; add margarine and pepper. Simmer uncovered for 5 minutes.

FRENCH ONION SOUP

Serves 4

3 T. no salt margarine
5 C. canned, less salt, beef broth
5 C. white onions, sliced thin
¼ tsp. pepper
1 tsp. Worcestershire sauce

In large non-stick saucepan, saute onions in margarine until tender. Add the beef broth to the onions with pepper and Worcestershire sauce. Cook, covered, on low for 35 minutes.

MIXED VEGETABLE SOUP

Serves 6

3 T. no salt margarine	2 large russet potatoes, scrubbed well and unpeeled, cut into ½" cubes
3 cloves garlic, minced	
4 C. clear, less salt, chicken broth	½ C. chopped parsley leaves
1-16 oz. can no salt tomatoes with juice, chopped	2 white onions, chopped
	2 C. shredded cabbage
	1 C. water
	2 C. frozen green peas
	¼ tsp. black pepper

Melt margarine in 3- to 4-quart saucepan. Add the onions and garlic; cook until tender. Add cabbage; cook 3 minutes. Mix the broth, water, tomatoes with juice and potatoes. Bring to boil, lower heat and simmer for 25 minutes or until potatoes are tender. Mix in peas, parsley and pepper. Simmer an additional 5 minutes.

DELIGHTFUL TURKEY SOUP

Serves 4

- 2 C. cooked turkey
- 2 white onions, diced
- 2 celery stalks, diced
- 1 C. egg noodles
- 1 C. fresh green peas
- 1/4 tsp. basil

- 6 C. turkey broth (you may also use clear, less salt, chicken broth)
- 3 carrots, diced
- 2 C. fresh mushrooms, sliced
- 1 C. broccoli pieces
- 1/8 C. dry white wine

With a knife, prepare vegetables. Place all ingredients except peas and broccoli in Dutch oven. Simmer 50 minutes. Add peas and broccoli and simmer 5 to 10 minutes more.

Code	Category	Code	Category
1100	Cookies	6100	Chinese Recipes
1200	Casseroles	6200	Danish Recipes
1300	Meat Dishes	6300	French Recipes
1400	Microwave	6400	German Recipes
1500	Cooking for "2"	6500	Greek Recipes
1600	Slow Cooking	6600	Hungarian Recipes
1700	Low Calorie	6700	Italian Recipes
1800	Canning & Freezing	6800	Irish Recipes
1900	Pastries & Pies	6900	Japanese Recipes
2000	Charcoal Grilling	7000	Mexican Recipes
2100	Appetizers	7100	Norwegian Recipes
2200	Beef	7200	Swedish Recipes
2300	Holiday Collection		
2400	Salads		
2500	Wild Game		
2600	Soups		
3100	Seafood & Fish		
3200	Poultry		
3300	My Own Recipes		
3400	Low Cholesterol		
3500	Chocoholic		
3600	Cooking with Wine		
3700	Cajun		
3800	Household Hints		

G & R PUBLISHING COMPANY

507 Industrial Street   Waverly, Iowa 50677

© Copyright 1982 G & R Publishing

Available Titles 01/90
Titles change without notice.   Printed U.S.A.